Nymans

West Sussex

THE NATIONAL TRUST

Nymans

Above A Red Admiral rests on a red dahlia

Nymans has grown into one of the great gardens of the Sussex Weald, thanks to four generations of the Messel family, their head gardeners and the National Trust:

1890–1915: Ludwig Messel laid out the framework of 'open-air rooms', and introduced rare magnolias and hybrid rhododendrons.

1915–53: Leonard and Maud Messel rebuilt the house in medieval style and planted more exotics and old roses.

1953–87: Their daughter, Anne Rosse, continued to enrich the garden after it was given to the National Trust in 1954.

1987–present day: Ludwig Messel's great-grandson, Alistair Buchanan, contributed to the garden's post-1987 restoration as family representative.

Right The magnificent herbaceous borders at Nymans abundant with floral colour

A Family View, by Alistair Buchanan

As a child, I used to hear my mother speak rapturously about Nymans. But I came to know the garden well only in the late 1970s, when trustee responsibilities brought me to see her cousin, Anne Rosse. Anne was a gifted visual gardener, as might be expected of the theatre designer Oliver Messel's sister. Vistas had been opened up and were focused by well-sited statues. 'Plant big, darling,' was her constant cry. Swathes of hydrangeas and camellias appeared, adding to the garden's colour and sense of intimacy. Her husband, Michael, was a scholarly gardener and encouraged the continued planting of rare trees and shrubs.

The National Trust was supportive at this period, but not innovative, as money was short. Fortunately, the garden was blessed with a team of skilled and dedicated gardeners. The first three Head Gardeners at Nymans, James Comber, Cecil Nice and David Masters, were all appointed Associates of Honour to the Royal Horticultural Society – a unique recognition.

By October 1987, Nymans was a vulnerable garden. The trees had not been thinned for two generations and had grown to great heights on relatively shallow soil and on the crest of a 500-foot ridge. On 15–16 October, 486 trees in the garden were blown down in the Great Storm. With exquisite timing, Anne Rosse had relinquished her role as garden director the previous day. I agreed to become family representative from that date.

We can look back now on a period of extraordinary progress. The hurricane allowed light into the garden. A new rose garden was planted, using cuttings from the old roses. A double perennial border was created in the Top Garden. The Pinetum was replanted and the National Trust has restored and opened the house. Visitor numbers have doubled, and Nymans is a beautiful place to be.

Left The Oliver Messel memorial in the Wall Garden in autumn

Ludwig Messel

Above Ludwig Messel

Right Ludwig Messel rebuilt the house and added a huge conservatory for tender exotics

Ludwig Messel was born in Darmstadt in central Germany in 1847, and by 1868 had settled in London, where he became a prosperous stockbroker. By 1890 he had six children and was looking for a country house in which to bring them up and enjoy a peaceful retirement. Like many at that period, he chose the Sussex Weald, buying a house and 600 acres at Nymans. He commissioned the fashionable architect Ernest George to extend the existing early 19th-century villa with a huge conservatory and an Italianate tower, which offered fine views over the narrow, wooded valley to the east and towards the Downs to the south.

The soil was a fertile, relatively frost-free loam over sandstone, and had already attracted many gardeners to the area, including Sir Edmund Loder at Leonardslee and the influential gardening writer William Robinson at Gravetye Manor. Both encouraged Messel to create a garden at Nymans, which got under way in earnest in September 1895, when the 29-year-old James Comber was appointed Head Gardener. Comber was a local man who had been trained at nearby Wakehurst Place and in the Veitch nurseries. His horticultural expertise and Messel's willingness to experiment with new plants were to prove the perfect combination.

One of their first major projects was the Pinetum, which was laid out in a horseshoe shape on an open slope to the north of the house. No fewer than fifteen varieties of *Pinus* and numerous other conifers offered a wide range of colour, shape and height. Most of their activity was, however, concentrated beyond the lawn to the south of the house. Here they created a rock garden of local sandstone planted up with helianthemums and dwarf shrubs such as cotoneaster. The nearby Heather Garden designed by Messel was one of the first of its kind, combining ericas with dwarf rhododendrons, all sheltered by *Pinus montana*. The Japanese Exhibition of 1903 inspired the pergola, over which were trailed *Wisteria sinensis* and *W. multijuga*. An avenue of limes linked the bottom of the Pinetum with the house and the Prospect,

a balustraded platform designed by Ludwig's architect brother Alfred.

The old orchard was transformed into the Wall Garden, which, because of its mild microclimate and particularly fertile soil, became a favourite site for tender exotics. Messel always preferred woody plants and shrubs, arranging magnolias and cherry trees along the drive with particular success. By 1916 there were over 80 species and more than 50 named hybrids of rhododendron at Nymans. Many of these came from the expeditions of the great plant-hunters such as Ernest 'Chinese' Wilson, whose most famous discovery, *Davidia involucrata* (the handkerchief tree), was grown at Nymans from 1908.

Above Ludwig Messel in his Pinetum

Above Ludwig Messel and his family on the Nymans lake. In the background is the picnic house

Left The Head Gardener James Comber (in bowler hat), with his son Harold and the garden staff at Nymans in 1909

5

Leonard and Maud Messel

Ludwig Messel's elder son Leonard had set up home with his wife Maud Sambourne, three miles from Nymans at Balcombe, where they created their own romantic garden. When Ludwig died in 1915, Maud was reluctant to move into the unwieldy Victorian mansion at Nymans. So in the 1920s it was transformed into a romantic medieval manor house. Tapestries were hung on limewashed walls, and oak Jacobean furniture was bought for the house.

While Leonard was serving in the First World War, his youngest sister Muriel looked after the garden, but died in the great flu epidemic of 1918. Maud created the Rose Garden, which she had planted with her favourite herbs and old-fashioned roses (then out of fashion), filling the house with their heady scent. It was also her idea to scatter bulbs beneath the maturing trees and shrubs for early spring colour.

Leonard Messel did not radically alter the framework of the garden devised by his father and James Comber, but he extended it north to form the Top Garden and developed a connoisseur's eye for a promising new rarity. He supported the great plant-hunters of the inter-war years, in particular Comber's son Harold, who brought back from his travels in Tasmania and the Andes such discoveries as *Alstroemeria ligtu angustifolia* 'Vivid', which was bred at Nymans from 1937. Like his father, Col. Messel was a shy man, but he was encouraged by his many gardening friends to begin exhibiting at the Royal Horticultural Society in 1923 – with immediate success. *Eucryphia* x *nymansensis* 'Nymansay' (actually entered, more prosaically, as 'Nymans A') received an Award of Merit in 1925 and a First Class Certificate in 1926. A succession of prize-winning magnolias, rhododendrons and camellias named after Nymans and its people followed.

By the 1930s, the garden had reached its peak and was regularly opened to the public, but all this came to an end with the Second World War. Fuel for the hot-houses disappeared, and the staff shrank from eleven to three elderly men. A further disaster struck on a freezing night in February 1947, when fire destroyed the house and, saddest of all, the Messels' irreplaceable botanical library. The garden, however, survived; indeed the wisteria that clambered through the open windows of the Great Hall only added to the romance

Above Magnolia 'Leonard Messel'

Right Leonard Messel with his daughter Anne

Above Maud Messel as a young woman

of the place. But the future of the garden remained uncertain. Leonard and Maud were in their seventies, and neither of their sons was interested in taking on the garden; their daughter Anne was, but she already had homes at Womersley in Yorkshire and Birr Castle in Co. Offaly to look after. So the family turned to the National Trust for help.

Left Wells the Butler in the Forecourt Garden after the fire in 1947

The National Trust and the Earl and Countess of Rosse

The great gardens of Britain had suffered even more than its country houses during the Second World War, and by 1947 the National Trust had been persuaded that they were just as worthy of preservation. Nymans was one of the first to come to the Trust, following Col. Messel's death in February 1953: for his funeral at St Mark's, Staplefield, the church was filled with evergreen foliage and hot-house lilies from Nymans, and the first of the spring flowers; James Comber died only three months later – in rhododendron time.

The early years of Trust ownership were not easy. Money was very short and sales from the kitchen garden, which should have supported the rest of the garden, were disappointingly low. But gradually the estate was put in order. The house was partially rebuilt and became the home of Anne and her second husband, Michael, 6th Earl of Rosse. The Head Gardener, Cecil Nice, who had lived for so long in the shadow of James Comber, continued to win prizes at the RHS, most famously perhaps with *Magnolia* x *loebneri* 'Leonard Messel'. A programme of plant exchanges with Birr Castle was set up, which brought many recent Chinese discoveries to Nymans.

By the 1960s, the planting was inevitably beginning to show its age, and the Trust's Gardens Adviser, Graham Stuart Thomas, decided to restock the Rose Garden with fresh plants and devise a new border to provide more interest in the Top Garden in June. Sadly, the labour-intensive kitchen garden had to be abandoned. With Lord Rosse's encouragement, the Woody Plant Catalogue was established to record the trees and shrubs at Nymans and other famous collections.

The Great Storm

During the night of 15–16 October 1987, hurricane-force winds swept across south-east England. On its hilltop site, Nymans was particularly vulnerable: the Pinetum, which had developed over almost a century, disappeared in a few hours. In all, Nymans lost 486 mature trees, including 20 of its champions and, worst of all, the giant Monkey Puzzle tree that symbolised Nymans for Anne Rosse. The Japanese pergola collapsed and many of the shrubs in the Wall Garden were smashed by falling trees.

David Masters, who had been appointed Head Gardener in 1980, and his team began the task of clearing up. But what of the future? The first priority was to restore the shelter belt which had given Nymans its mild climate, and to reinstate the Pinetum, choosing species characteristic of the garden, many taken from cuttings off fallen trees. The Great Storm provided opportunities as well as difficulties: many of the trees lost were past their best and had been robbing the shrubs and borders of light and water; gardens can never stand still, and there was now a chance for a more radical rethink. So the Rose Garden has been replanted using new trellises, but with the same old-fashioned roses Maud Messel had favoured. Within the overall plan laid out by Ludwig Messel, the famous collection of foreign plants is also being enriched with new introductions. Nymans enters its second century in good heart.

Above Alfred Messel's garden temple in the Pinetum before the storm

Left Nymans and the Pinetum after the storm

Opposite (from left to right) Lord and Lady Rosse and Head Gardener Cecil Nice, in 1975

The House

Above The Book Room

Above The Library

Three generations of the Messel family have lived at Nymans, but the present house reflects most strongly the taste of Col. Leonard Messel and his wife Maud. They had three children: Linley, who joined the family stockbrockers; Anne, who was one of the great beauties of the 1920s and '30s; and Oliver, the most creative theatre designer of his day, whose artistic talents were inherited by his nephew, Lord Snowdon, and grand-nephew, Lord Linley.

Leonard inherited in 1915 and decided almost at once to pull down the Victorian house, although it was only 25 years old. Maud was the daughter of *Punch*'s political cartoonist Linley Sambourne and herself an artist with a wide knowledge of architecture. She toured the West Country seeking inspiration from ancient manor houses like Great Chalfield Manor in Wiltshire. The photographs and sketches she made on these trips were the starting point for the architects
Sir Walter Tapper and Norman Evill, who began work on the new house in 1923, very much under her guidance. *Country Life*'s architectural writer Christopher Hussey described the result, which was finally completed in 1928, as 'so clever a reproduction ... of a building begun in the 14th century and added to intermittently until Tudor times, that some future antiquary may well be deceived by it'.

The limewashed walls and old oak panelling provided an appropriately plain background for the Messels' collection of 17th-century furniture, pictures, tapestries and porcelain. According to Hussey, Mrs Messel possessed 'a charming taste,

directing everything from the components and treatment of rooms down to the choice of furniture and arrangement of flowers'. The Library held the great collection of botanical books assembled by Leonard and his father, which was tragically destroyed by the fire of 1947. Paradoxically, this disaster has given the ruined house an even greater air of romantic antiquity.

After the fire, the Messels moved to Holmsted Manor nearby, and the surviving north-east end was repaired as a base from which to run the garden. Although the decorated plaster ceilings were lost, enough furniture and other objects were salvaged to reproduce, on a smaller scale, the character of the rooms before the fire. More were brought down following the sale of the family's London house in Lancaster Gate.

After Maud Messel died in 1960, her daughter Anne took over the running of the garden, although she stayed here only occasionally when she wanted to entertain her friends from the horticultural world; she called it her 'potting shed'. Anne Rosse hated any notion of conventional 'good taste', but she respected the past, leaving untouched the late 19th-century interior of her grandfather's house in Stafford Terrace, which was passed to the Victorian Society. So while Nymans today is full of mementoes of Anne and her brother Oliver Messel (who made the television set in the form of a miniature theatre), it remains very much as it was in their parents' day.

Lady Rosse died at Nymans in 1992, and thanks to the family's generosity the house can now be enjoyed by the public.

Opposite The Garden Hall

Tour of the Garden

Above View from the Pinetum across the Sussex Weald

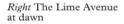

Right The Lime Avenue at dawn

Opposite The Garden Temple in the snow

1 **The Pinetum**

The two giant redwoods are almost the sole survivors of the Great Storm of 1987 which destroyed the old Pinetum. The new Pinetum was planted in April 1990 in the shape of a horseshoe surrounding the meadow, which is covered with daffodils in spring. The grass is left uncut until late summer allowing the wild flowers and their attendant populations of insects to flourish. Over 150 varieties of conifer have been planted, many propagated from those lost in the storm. Maples, eucryphia and birch trees have been interplanted with the conifers, together with beds of hydrangea and Pampas grass. The garden temple was designed by Alfred Messel in 1907.

In the lower Pinetum, a series of enigmatic, abstract box topiary forms leads into a davidia glade. Once mature, this dense planting of the Ghost Tree, *Davidia involucrata*, will form an extraordinary canopy of pure white 'handkerchiefs' when the trees flower.

2 **The Lime Avenue**

From here views can be enjoyed over the Nymans parkland and woods. Across the valley are the Balcombe water-tower, High Beeches clock-tower and the red-brick Ditton Place. At the bottom of the park is an arboretum, containing many unusual trees, which may be visited on the woodland walks.

Running parallel to the avenue is the Laurel Walk.

Above Kniphofia uvaria nobilis (Red-Hot Poker)

Left The Sunk Garden is thickly planted with cannas and geraniums

3 The Prospect

Passing by the original main entrance to the house you will reach the Prospect from where you will have splendid views out over the woods, which can be entered via a gate at the extreme south-east corner of the garden.

Crossing the Laurel Walk, which is interplanted with *Laburnum* 'Vossii', takes you on to the Lawn (8).

4 The Sunk Garden

An Istrian marble Byzantine urn is the centrepiece for displays of bedding, which are planted for spring and summer effect, using a varying range of annuals, half-hardy perennials and bulbs. The surrounding 'hedge' of camellias was grown from cuttings brought from America by Lord and Lady Rosse in the 1960s. The summer-house or loggia was built in the 1920s and was used by the family for picnics and storing tennis equipment. The walls are covered with the rose 'Dundee Rambler' and *Clematis* x *jackmanii*.

5 The Tennis Lawn

Formerly used for playing tennis by the family, the lawn is now surrounded by plantings of seasonal interest. On the east side a border planted for mainly blue and silver effect contains plants such as ceanothus, agapanthus, hibiscus, artemisia and olearia. A large *Magnolia sargentiana robusta*, which is covered with large pink blossoms in spring and scarlet fruits in autumn, is underplanted with colchicum.

The mound of rhododendrons to the south contains several old varieties such as 'Cynthia'. Nearby stands a *Liriodendron chinense*. To the west is a border containing large plants of *Magnolia* x *soulangeana* and *M. denudata* surrounded by buddleia, potentilla, cytisus, cortaderia and kniphofia.

Opposite The Tennis Lawn with magnolia

The Wild Garden

Across the main Handcross–Staplefield road are the Wild Garden and the Rhododendron Wood. Originally part of the garden nurseries, this area had become overgrown by the 1970s. Following the Great Storm, much clearance work has been carried out and a large number of rare and interesting trees planted, including *Castanopsis cuspidata*, a champion tree from Japan and Korea, and *Maytenus boaria*. These, we hope, will grow into beautiful maturity with the rest of the 'New Nymans'.

Woodland Walks

The majority of the woodland at Nymans lies in the valley below the garden. This is one of the most delightful areas of the estate as well as being one of the least well known. Three signed Woodland Walks now run through these woods. These allow visitors the opportunity to see some of the fine trees in the arboretum at the bottom of the parkland, bluebells in abundance in springtime, the tallest tree in Sussex and the large lake, once a medieval hammer pond lying at the foot of the valley.

Above The Wild Garden

Right The woodland walks are carpeted in bluebells in May

Above Poppies in the borders in June

Right Cornus kousa

Far right Close up of *Davidia* 'Golden Birr'

Opposite Galanthus nivalis in the Top Garden

13 The Top Garden

The path from the Rose Garden towards the entrance leads to the Top Garden. The straight path is flanked by the June Borders. As the name implies, these have been planted primarily for interest in June, using plants such as lupins, delphinium, oriental poppies, roses, deutzia and philadelphus.

The winding path to the left by the green shed takes you past a quarry where the sandstone for the original paths was quarried. It is planted with *Gunnera manicata*, which in one season produces leaves of up to two metres across. The first frosts of autumn cause the leaves to blacken and collapse. Near the quarry is a *Meliosma veitchiorum* grown from seed collected in China by E.H. Wilson. At over fifteen metres, it is as tall as any that Wilson would have seen in the wild. The large, pinnate leaves turn a glorious butter-yellow in autumn.

The northern half of the Top Garden is centered on an area of grass which is surrounded by trees and shrubs. These include *Magnolia* 'Leonard Messel', which was raised at Nymans, with its two parents, *Magnolia kobus* and *M. stellata* 'Rosea', standing nearby. Several *Cornus kousa* appear to be snow-laden in mid-summer, when their branches are covered in white bracts, followed in autumn by strawberry-like fruits.

Newer plantings include *Sorbus* 'Joseph Rock', *Davidia* 'Golden Birr', *Rhododendron* 'Philip Holmes' and a sorbus planted in memory of Cecil Nice, gardener and Head Gardener at Nymans from 1924 to 1980.

Left A 'Fritz Nobis' rose

Opposite The path through the Rose Garden

Above An 'Henri Martin' moss rose

12 The Rose Garden

There has been a rose garden on this site since the 1920s, when Maud Messel planted a fine collection of old-fashioned varieties, many of them given to her by Ellen Willmott, as well as collected from French and Italian gardens.

In 1987 it was decided to renovate this area. The roses had grown tired with age and were starved of light by the over-shadowing trees. The paths were also no longer able to cope with the increased number of visitors. During the winter of 1988–9 a new layout was constructed and new arches and pillars installed. Over 150 varieties of 'old-fashioned' roses have been planted. Vivien ap Rhys Pryce designed a fountain in the form of a bronze rose, to provide a focus of light and movement at the centre of the new garden.

11 The Wall Garden

This is the heart of Nymans. It was the first part of the garden laid out by Ludwig Messel and is a treasure house of beautiful and rare plants.

The central paths meet at an Italian fountain carved from Verona red marble, which is flanked by fine topiary yew globes. In summer the borders are filled with a riot of colourful annuals and perennials backed by shrubs to give height and a feeling that one is walking along a corridor of colour. Summer-flowering trees include *Styrax hemsleyanus*, *S. japonicus*, *Chionanthus virginicus*, halesia and *Magnolia sieboldii*, *M.* x *soulangeana* and *M. liliiflora*. One large *Eucryphia* x *nymansensis* survives of those raised at Nymans around the time of the First World War.

In spring the grassy areas are full of bulbs, primarily narcissi, but also thousands of Snakes Head 'Fritillary' (*Fritillaria meleagris*) and erythroniums. Above are large magnolias – *M.* 'Charles Raffill', *M. sargentiana*, *M. campbellii* and *M.* 'Cecil Nice'.

Around the perimeter are borders containing a collection of plants from South America, primarily Chile. Some of them are original plants grown from seed collected by the Head Gardener James Comber's son Harold in Chile and Argentina in the 1920s. These have been supplemented by younger plants grown from seed collected in recent years in Chile by Martin Gardner and Sabina Knees.

Left The Italian marble fountain at the middle of the Wall Garden

Overleaf A cherry tree (*Prunus* × *subhirtella* 'Rosea') in the Wall Garden in spring

Above Hydrangea petiolaris drapes a doorway to the Wall Garden

Above Snakes Head 'Fritillary' photographed in spring

25

Right Pink camellias
flowering in the Forecourt

Below right The dovecote
also provides shelter to
climbing white roses

9 The Forecourt

This walled garden with the dovecote in
one corner was carefully restored in 1966
following photographs published in *Country
Life* in 1932. It contains many aromatic and
slightly tender plants, including Dutch
lavender, cistus, teucrium and artemisia.
Four standard bay trees are being trained
into the shape of mushrooms.

Once the private garden of Lady
Rosse, this area is now tended by Alistair
Buchanan continuing the family
involvement with Nymans.

10 The Knot Garden

Another new planting for 1996, the box
edging encloses dianthus, hermerocallis,
delphiniums, lupins and Rose 'Nathalie
Nypels'. The garden is flanked on two sides
by the 'toblerone' yew hedge.

Opposite The dovecote in
the Forecourt

8 The Lawn

Overlooking the Lawn are the ruins of the house built by Col. and Mrs Messel in the 1920s. The ruins play host to many climbing plants, including *Lonicera etrusca* 'Michael Rosse', clematis, wisteria and roses. The border plants include melianthus, romneya, artemisia, the roses 'Penelope' and 'Felicia', osteospermums and peonies.

The large Cedar of Lebanon, copper beech and cryptomeria were the sole survivors of the Great Storm. The Monkey Puzzle tree was destroyed, as were a very fine Deodar Cedar and the Morinda Spruce. A young Monkey Puzzle tree was planted by Lady Rosse to signal the start of the replanting of Nymans, and a young Deodar and two Lebanon Cedars have also been introduced.

The semicircular beds contain fuchsias. On the roadside are banks of rhododendrons and *Hydrangea* 'Générale Vicomtesse de Vibraye'. They face banks of bird cherry with *Hydrangea* 'Blue Wave' and H. 'Madame Emile Mouillière'.

A feature at the northern end of the Lawn is a basket of winter jasmine filled with red-flowered hydrangeas representing fruit. Nearby is a bed of 'London Pride' with the original *Magnolia* 'Anne Rosse' at its centre.

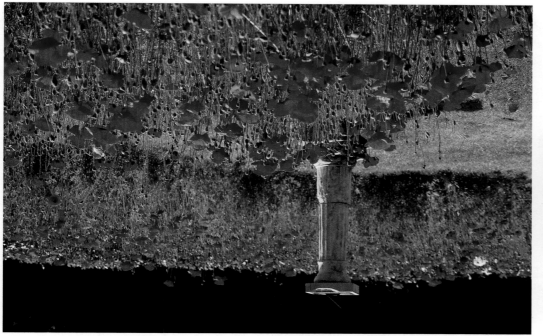

Above Cedars of Lebanon on the Main Lawn

Right Sundial amidst a host of Ladybird Poppies

Above The Ginger Lily

6 The Heather Garden

This forms the southern limit of the garden with views to the South Downs and Balcombe Viaduct to the south-east. It was one of the first heather gardens to be laid out in England and was originally planned by Ludwig Messel around a hillock, giving the advantage of different levels. Meandering grass paths divide a series of large beds, which contain a variety of heathers and many rhododendrons grown from seed collected by the plant-hunters George Forrest, Frank Kingdon-Ward and Joseph Rock; particularly notable are *Rh. cerasinum* KW5830 and *saluenense* R59194. There is also a considerable group of *Pieris japonica* (including a large variegated example), hakea, embothrium and berberis.

7 The Croquet Lawn and Pergola

The Lawn is overlooked by a mount topped by a wooden structure, through which a weeping hornbeam is growing. From the top are fine views over the Heather Garden and further afield to the South Downs. Its banks are planted with cistus, hebe, pines, junipers and polygonum, which cascades down into the border below, where it is interplanted with bergenia.

On the west side of the Croquet Lawn is the Pergola, built in 1903. It was damaged in the 1987 storm, when several piers fell, and the wisteria, specially imported from Japan in 1904, which the Pergola supports, was badly damaged. Rebuilt during the winter of 1989–90, it has been planted with young wisteria, clematis and rambler roses, with creamy-white *Hydrangea arborescens* 'Grandiflora' alongside and *Iris sibirica* next to the lawn.

On the north side of the Lawn are rhododendrons, a large group of *Pieris formosa* var. *forrestii* cv. 'Wakehurst' and new plantings of heathers. The stone lanterns at each corner of the lawn were acquired from the 1903 Japanese Exhibition in London.

Left The Pagoda at the Croquet Lawn

Left A Japanese lantern with a bed of irises in the foreground

Above Wisteria smothers the Pergola in June